Living Within a Strange Mind

Volume Two

Jim West

Foreword

I guess life is as unexpected as anything can be. Over the years, I've made and lost so many friends. Some due to moving away, some due to a change of social status. Some due to a change in philosophy.

It's just part of life. But, there's always been those friends that stood by my side regardless of the miles, or the changes in either of our lives.

I'm not sure why some of them have stuck with me for so many years. Maybe just to see what happens next. Or what I'll say or do that proves my erratic nature.

It doesn't matter. Good friends are one of the blessings of life. Next to a good wife or husband, they're the most important things in your world. Besides your kids--but they have to love you--it's the law. Maybe even a constitutional amendment or one of the less important articles. I know it's there somewhere.

Anyway, I suppose you read Volume 1 and just wanted to see what else was rattling around in the vacant areas of my head. However you came to be holding this book, I'm glad you are, and I hope some of the little verses within will touch you. Or bring back a fond memory.

As always, keep your mouth closed, your mind and your ears open, and smile at life as if you hadn't a care in the world. Life is easier when you refrain from stupid things. And it's sometimes, but not always, hard to do stupid things when you keep quiet and pay attention to those around you.

As Lao Tzu said, "An uneaten hamburger tastes the same as an uneaten lobster." Wait, I don't think that was Lao Tzu. Could have been me.

One

Tumbling through crevasses hewn from aged rock and spreading across the endless plains, a sparkling river surges. All forms of life come forth as she flows from the mountains, and a melody of songs spring loose as the clear blue waters caress the pebbles and embrace the boulders.

Flowing deep and tireless, she rolls and bubbles toward the sea. Framed by magnificent forests, meandering beside waving grass and blossoming flowers, she varies from melancholy to vibrant, instilling such peacefulness yet capable of exciting the tumultuous feelings from deep within my heart.

She changes along with the seasons, seeming to gain more beauty with each. In the spring, the multitude of fragrant hues from the budding flowers seems to be absorbed by her rippling waters. As fall arrives, the rusty red and golden leaves are reflected across her face in a blaze of glory.

Through the years, she subtly shifts her course, following the various curves of the earth and molding herself around each obstacle. Everywhere she wanders, she blesses her banks with abundant life and surrenders her evaporating waters for gentle rains that bring exquisite beauty miles away.

I yearn to drink from her quenching depths and to bathe in her cooling waters that cleanse the body and soothe the soul. I dream of floating along with her as she continues onward. To enjoy the turbulent rapids, to lie peacefully as she rolls softly through the prairies. I want to remain with her until she finally enters the sea, and only her wondrous memory remains.

Two

You really thought you knew me,
You thought you knew me well.
But everything you thought you knew,
Was only what I would tell.

I kept most everything,
Close within my mind.
Private thoughts I hid so deep,
These thoughts you'd never find.

The outer things I let you see,
But not what's in my heart.
Just smiles and jokes and witty talk,
You only saw that part.

For years and years, you only saw,
Just what I'd want you to.
The deeper thoughts I sealed away,
To hide them all from you.

I found it hard to show the things,
That you so wanted to know.
I couldn't let you see these things,
I couldn't let them show.

I wish I could be different,
I wish I could have shown.
But I didn't or couldn't,
These thoughts are mine alone.

Three

I wonder if she knows how much I love her.

Does she know I see her face in the glow of the early morning light as the sun paints the sky with vibrant colors? As the wispy clouds spread the hues across the broad horizon?

Does she know that I can feel her when the warmth of the day surrounds me? A warmth that sinks through my body as the sun shines on my face after the chill of the evening is over?

Does she know how the soft billowing clouds of pure white remind me of the gentle way she touches me? Of the security and serenity that wraps me in a cloak of downy firmness?

Does she know that the majesty of a snow-capped mountain resembles her statuesque beauty? The awe I feel when I see her deep within herself? The security she gives me, knowing that she is always there even when her mind is elsewhere?

Does she know how the gentle rains cool me and give me renewed faith? How the sparkling drops of rain spread the rainbow of beauty through me, as she does when I see her?

Does she know that I see her in the meadows of waving grass and blossoming flowers? How the feeling of vibrant life flows through me as I see the magnificent colors blend in such a panorama of peaceful beauty?

Does she know how every minute of every day, the beauty of this world, brings her to my mind? From the soft buds of springtime to the solid permanence of a mountain range draped with towering pine? From the unfathomable depths of the oceans to the gentle breeze that caresses me?

I wonder if she knows?

Four

You turned your head so slightly,
And then you looked at me.
Your brightly shining eyes,
Were so very plain to see.

You smiled at me and nodded,
And then you turned away.
But that first glimpse of you,
Forever in my mind would stay.

I thought that you were lovely,
You looked so very sweet.
I knew that you were the one,
I really had to meet.

I stood there so quietly,
My mind was fairly numb.
Everything I thought to say,
I knew would sound so dumb.

Again, you turned to me,
And I saw your pretty smile.
But my feet were stuck there, frozen,
This could take a while.

The years have all flown past,
That was so long ago.
But now, you're here with me,
And I know you've loved me so.

Five

I just can't imagine,
Not having you in my life.
I don't think I could make it,
If you were not my wife.

After all these years,
All the give and take.
You're the best decision,
I've ever had to make.

And just now, as you turned,
And you looked at me again.
I saw, just like the first time,
And again, you made me grin.

Until my time is over,
Until the day I die.
My mind will still remember,
The love that's in your eye.

Happy Anniversary Darling

Six

The shadows grow long and deep into the night. They move with a life far beyond my worst nightmares. Daggers of darkness intent on heinous acts.

I retreat from the gloom cast by the intrusion of some object into the faint glow of the moon. A cloud drifts across the pale light, exploding the shadows into grotesque figures. All of my light is disappearing, the, shadows are coming closer. I try to hide from them, but they are relentless.

My light was so precious. It filled me with such joy and kept the shadows away. Now, they are intruding further and further into my life, my light. I seem powerless to prevent it.

It is almost complete. They have stretched almost to where I cower beside the wall. There is nowhere to run or hide. Only the occasional brilliance of a passing beam drives them back, but only for the briefest of moments. They return so quickly, so eager to reach me and shroud me in darkness. There is no evading them now.

Continued

In the far distance, I see a faint shimmering. A ray of hope! It moves toward me, but ever so slowly. I want to dash toward it, but my leaden legs refuse to obey.

I know this light! It had been beside me for so long. There to hold me in its warmth. How did it get so far away?

I try to call out! The dryness of charred cotton fills my mouth. A coppery bile rises in my throat and chokes me. I can feel my heart racing, the valves slamming shut as adrenalin courses through my veins.

How did I ever get so far from my light? What could have drawn me into this fearful abyss? How could I have let the glimmer of other flickering candles entice me to leave the secure warmth of my light? What a fool I must have been. Now, I'm stranded here. Surrounded by the razor-edged shadows. They grow even darker, more menacing. I plead with the distant light to come. Just a small glow for me to remain in.

But it is too late. As I watch helplessly, the last remaining hope fades with the dying of the light. Now, nothing but the oppressing darkness surrounds me. The shadows slash into my soul.

I am Lost Forever.

Seven

There was an old black man,

I knew so long ago.

His memory has stayed with me,

As down life's road I go.

I never saw his color,

I only saw his heart.

We always worked together,

And he always did his part.

A man who works beside you,

And truly earns his pay.

That's a man I'll standby,

And work with every day.

Because work has no color,

And neither does your pride.

Just give me a hard worker,

To stand close by my side.

This old black man has taught me,

As much as had my Dad,

To have known this gentleman,

I am truly glad.

Now, I just wonder,

If he was still living here,

All the things that he would see,

Would they break a heart so dear?

Continued

When a man uses his color,
And that's his only excuse.
To shun from work and labor,
Of him, I have no use.

That old black man I once knew,
From years now, long past.
He gave me my beliefs,
And through these years, they last.

Never think about the color,
Just try to see the man.
If he works there beside you,
And does the best he can.

But if he's just plain lazy,
Or wants a ride that's free.
Color still doesn't matter,
It's a worthless man, you see.

Eight

Death is but a wish. It comes so late in life. But, sometimes, it hurries and lays its cold fingers upon your shoulders so softly. Sometimes, it lingers closely and waits for you to ask. But it's always there to speed you on when the time has come.

Often, now I see it and want it to come to me. I ask for some mercy and help to speed me away. I've lived my life and seen so much. I dread what lies ahead. The ravages of old age now lay their cold hands upon me. I want to go while I have my mind and leave no problems for those left behind.

I want my children to see me as I once was to them. Remember me as the man who ran, who lived my life so full. Take me now and spare my kids of what now lies ahead. Send me to that other place where those like me now reside. Let the ones I leave behind remember me with pride.

Don't make me lay in old, soiled sheets with tubes and constant care. Let me take my dignity and determine my own fate. While I'm still alive and useful to others, let me leave the memory of one who cared and gave to them. Let me go with some grace.

Death is not the enemy. It's really my best friend. He takes me when I need to go and gives the final end.

Nine

Trust is such a fragile thing,
It really doesn't die.
But you can easily kill it,
Even if you don't try.

You don't have to lie to do it,
Just not saying what is true.
Like not telling all the parts,
That's all you have to do.

Once you lose the trust you had,
It's probably gone forever.
Though you try to get it back,
The answer's usually never.

And without another's trust,
That's the way you have to live.
Because if your word is useless,
You've nothing else to give.

So always strive to keep your word,
And honor every trust.
Because to really be a man,
That's one thing that's a must.

Ten

The old house sat there, much as I remembered it. Quietly waiting for those who had shared its rooms and walls. Remembering the things that had been there so many years ago.

Its windows coated with the grime of time. The paint now faded and chipped, showing the ravages of time. Harsh winds and unrelenting sun sapping the life from my home.

The years have passed, and I've aged too. As much as the old home. The colors have faded, and lines now show up on the exterior of my soul.

The things I've seen have hollowed my heart like the empty rooms. The cracks of the windowpanes distort the light much as my eyes now see the fragments of my life.

When left alone, time is not a friend. Constant care, a new coat of paint, or wool are the things that are necessary to make us feel renewed. Someone to want to live within our old homes, our old souls.

How I want to go back, to feel the joy of that old home. To see its windows glowing from within, shining with the light of love.

Eleven

Sometimes, a man must make a choice,
When neither one seems clear.
But a decision must be made,
You choose the best one there.

And if things don't work out right,
Just do the best you can.
You can't blame another one,
You must face it like a man.

Wisdom comes from living,
And sometimes being wrong.
But when you admit your failures,
You end up twice as strong.

Being wrong every now and then,
No matter how hard you try.
Is just another fact of life,
Until the day you die.

But admitting when you've been wrong,
And try to make it right.
You'll make this world a better place,
And it lets you sleep at night.

If you're ever wrong again,
And always have an excuse.
You never stand and take the blame,
Of you, I have no use.

Twelve

Free? Do you really think so? Can you come and go whenever you want? Wherever you want? I think not.

Can you leave your home, your work, your family? Can you walk away and not worry about any of it?

Who will pay the bills you leave behind? Who will pay the bills you gather along the way?

If you are truly free, why do you have to do these things? Why are you bound by things stronger than the bars of a prison?

Free? Is your mind free? Can you think of only what you want? Or must you think of others and other things?

I don't think we're ever free. Our parents control us in our youth. Our debts control us in the middle years. Society controls us through it all. Truly free?

I don't think so.

Thirteen

Ode to Don Jackson

He was a mild-mannered fellow,
With an easygoing style.
Sometimes, he was charming,
With a real infectious smile.

He was a man eager to learn,
All the new-fangled ways.
Always listening to the others,
Especially from the olden days.

He started hearing about a new disease,
The one they called 'Mad Cow'.
Lots of cattle could get it,
But he didn't know just how.

So he asked an old cowhand,
He'd known since just a pup.
Asked if he'd heard about it,
And what was really up.

The old man scratched his head,
And gave him a big grin.
"Sure," he said,
"Once I had one penned."

Continued

"He was shore a biggun',
A big ol' Brangus bull.
I had him in a corner,
Cause the sorting pen was full."

"He'd snort and paw,
With all the strength he had.
Now I'll tell you, son,
That cow was really mad!"

Fourteen

The storm came charging in from the west,
Bringing thunder, wind, rain, and the rest.
I sat behind the glass, watching it arrive,
Just sitting there watching, so glad to be alive.

Clouds, tall, monstrous, and dark,
Whipping up grass, stripping trees of their bark.
The winds howling across all of the land,
Trees finally falling, unable to still stand.

The rain pelted all as deafening thunder crashed,
The night lit up as lightning bolts flashed.
Outside people ducking, as for cover they ran,
Pelted by torrents, scurrying as fast as they can.

The power of the storm, all around us it, grew,
When it would stop, nobody knew.
The forces of nature, bringing its wrath from the sky,
Some safe and warm, while others must die.

As the windows shook from the force of the storm,
I sat there watching, very dry and warm.
It raged outside, and me just sitting in the room,
Anxiously awaiting--- the next crashing boom.

Damn, I love a good storm.

Fifteen

Time is our only true treasure, time with our friends and family, time to enjoy. Of all the things we hold dear, it's the only thing that we can control but never renew. Once time runs out, there is never anymore.

Cherish each moment of the time you have with those who mean the most to you. Their time on earth is limited, and so is yours. Spend those precious moments with them, even if it's only in your thoughts.

Never waste a second on those that mean so little in the grand scheme of life. Don't dwell on past grievances or things you can't control. If you wouldn't spend your money on them, why would you waste that which is much more valuable?

Always remember the things that brought you joy and keep them in the forefront of your mind. Make sure you save those moments and release all others. Unhappy thoughts waste time better spent on those that make you smile.

Should you lose money, you can make more. Should you lose any other object, it can be replaced. Should you lose time, it is gone forever. It must be spent wisely, invested only in those things that bring happiness for the measured days you have left.

Share your time. Spend it with those who enjoy your company. For every moment spent with a fool, not only is your time wasted, but so is that of those who want to be with you. Tell those near you how much you miss them when you're apart. Keep them forever in your memories. As you lay down for your final rest, don't be sorry you missed any opportunity for happiness.

Your time has expired.

Sixteen

I told you goodbye today,
We both knew it was the end.
But you're such a special person,
And you'll always be my friend.

We've been so close for some time now,
And shared our lives from day to day.
We've always held each other close,
But we both knew one would go away.

I watched you leave this morning,
And as you drove away,
I felt a part of me dying,
But here I had to stay.

We both saw the problems,
That would always be around.
And thought that just our love,
Would make them come unwound.

But, finally, we've had to face it,
The distance between us too great.
The miles, the age, the needs of life,
Meant we'd never mate.

Through it all, and even now,
Though my heart is breaking.
I'll always remember you,
As a chance well worth taking.

I will love you forever.

Seventeen

The old pickup crunched to a halt, raising dust from the gravel road
that led to a weathered old ranch house in the distance.
Stooped and bent by many years of work and toil,
the tired old rancher slid his frail body from the sagging seat
as the hinges screeched and protested the door's opening.

Ambling to the battered and rusting mailbox,
He watched a distant red-tailed hawk
swoop low across the empty pasture
beyond the ancient, sagging, barbed wire fence
in search of a tidbit of unwary rabbit or mouse.

Tugging open the box's bent and weathered door,
He awaited with anticipation for some small spark of joy.
Peering inside, disappointment showed as he pushed it closed
on the emptiness inside both the box and
his hopes of some smidgen of attention or care.

Solemnly shaking his down fallen head,
He pulled the brim of his sweat-stained old hat
lower over his eyes and returned
to his ancient yet waiting truck,
still idling amidst the lingering dust of his dreams.

Now, slowly driving down the road to his lonely house,
the empty pastures reminded him of his life in these final years.
They remained just as the hollow emptiness of the mailbox.
Those things that bring joy and happiness are now
so few and so very, very far between.

Eighteen

For some, each day slowly drifts into the next.
Sliding through the week, months, and years
Without interruption or consciousness of
The value of each one.

They fail to see each day as an opportunity.
A new chance to see the wonders
Of the world that surrounds them
Or all of the joys that await.

Never taking time to enjoy a moment in the sun,
Feeling the softness of rain on your face,
Or tasting the cool wetness of a snowflake
When you catch it on your tongue.

Foregoing the warmth of friendship or family,
Not realizing that these are the things
That make every moment of your life
The only things worth living.

Look anew upon those things that make you happy.
Find the beauty of everyday life with friends.
At the end of our short time here on earth,
These are truly the only things with meaning.

Relish the touch of a lover's hand.
Bask in the joy of a child's smile.
Cherish each moment you live.
Today may be the last one you have.

Nineteen

So many times, there are so many choices we must make. Which road will take us to where we want to be? Each of these roads has different characteristics. Some are paved, some gravel, and some are dirt. You make your choice every time you come to an intersection. Everyone makes their choice as they reach that point. Every choice leads you somewhere.

Sometimes, it's where you don't want to be. But you may not know that when you start down the road. However, there's always another path along the way. A path that leads you back in the direction you desired if you'll just take it.

Most people see the smooth paved road and know it would be easier to travel. Some will forego the dirt path because it looks like it may have ruts. Some bypass the gravel because it looks rough. Only a few will travel these more difficult passages. It may be a sense of adventure or possibly because they wandered off their path due to inattention or a lack of vision.

A man has choices every day. The choice to go in any direction he wants. The measure is how many times he chooses the right path or how he corrects those he made wrong. The end isn't written. It changes each day as we weigh the value of the options presented.

Even after hundreds of missteps, there's always a path that will lead you home.

Just take it.

Twenty

I'm not gone, not really.
Yea, though I'm no longer here,
The part of me that matters
Here, it still remains.

The small things I've owned,
The shirt I wore, the hat,
The spurs, the boots,
They hold most of me.

Every time you see these things,
You'll see me.
Every time you touch them,
You'll be touching me.

Twenty-One

There's a lot of things I want to say,
But I can't say them all.
I want to say I love you,
But I say nothing at all.

If you'd just look,
And use just not your ears.
You'd see I've always loved you,
Through all these long, long years.

Though I said goodbye,
So many years ago.
I've held you in my heart,
And really loved you so.

Twenty-Two

Sometimes, someone says something,
Be it family or friend.
That brings a certain joyous feeling,
And seems to never end.

A small smile, so very, very small,
Most would hardly see.
It resides deep within your heart,
Just between you and me.

But every time you think of it,
Again comes the smile.
The memory floods your heart and soul,
For just a little while.

Days and weeks go flowing by,
Without this thought inside.
But suddenly, it comes again,
Then, a grin, a touch of pride.

But those that truly know you,
See it cross your face.
They know not to ask you why,
It's just not their place.

You never say a single word,
It's not for them to see.
Cause 'tis just between us two,
Meant for you and me.

Twenty-Three

It's been rumored that the Universe is vast,
But mine is very small.
There's no billions and billions of distant stars,
There is just you, that's all.

Maybe mine's not so very real,
In the grand scheme of things.
Cause my life revolves around so little,
Like the joy that memory brings.

If I were to try and see,
The world that's outside of mine.
And if it all just went away,
With you, I'd be just fine.

As long as you're still around this ol' world,
My universe will keep its place.
Because every time I see the stars,
I'll always see your face.

Twenty-Four

There are those that fight,
And those that refrain.
There are those that die,
And those that remain.

There are those that know,
Why so many others died.
And the ones left behind,
For loved ones, they cried.

But there are some,
That don't know the cost,
Or what they would lose,
If the battles had been lost.

Those that look down
On the brave ones that went,
While they stayed home,
Cursing the money they had spent.

To support the brave ones,
That took the battle far away.
To protect another's rights,
To say what they want to say.

They have no honor,
They have no pride,
But I will stay forever,
With brave men by my side.

Twenty-Five

Keep me not in your hands,
But deep within your heart.
Your hands hold so little,
While your heart is the greater part.

Your hands may hold a trinket,
The heart's vastness is immense.
So keep the memories you cherish,
And always remember me hence.

Twenty-Six

A man's life is complex,
Things always need consideration.
How to keep everything steady,
And maintain moderation.

Many things are always present,
Keeping appearance just to start.
Trying to seem viral,
Trying to appear smart.

How many dollars do you make?
What kind of car do you drive?
What kind of job do you have?
It's hard to just be alive.

Not to mention sex,
Can you still stand the measure,
Or do the younger guys,
Get access to the treasure.

Twenty-Seven

T'is there a heaven?
That I do not know.
T'is there a hell?
That I know not either.

When I go,
Just where I go,
I'm sure that's
Where I'll be.

A voice in the wind,
A shadow on the wall,
All there so
You'll remember me.

Twenty-Eight

I met a lady I thought perfect,
At least, so it seemed to me.
But she belonged to another,
So, for me, she couldn't be.

For quite some time, I watched their lives,
To learn what I would see.
And when I saw how she really was,
Made me feel sorry for he.

Poor Bastard!

Twenty-Nine

Cats in the Moonlight,
Eyes locked on something.
Quietly sitting,
Tails slowly switching.

Nothing else moving.
Eyes just yellow slits glowing.
Never blinking, never wavering,
Patiently sitting, calmly waiting.

Unmoved by the world around them,
Concentration unshaken,
Constantly judging,
Condemnation, they're taken.

Then they blink and walk away.

Thirty

I held your hand when you were small,
You pulled and ran away.
I just wanted to hold you,
You just wanted to play.

I held your hand a few years later,
And you pulled away as you grew.
I just wanted to hold you,
But you wanted something new.

I held your hand when you were older,
But again, you just let go.
As much as I wanted to hold you,
You just wanted to grow.

I held your hand at the alter,
Then gave it to another.
I gave you to a man,
You loved like no other.

Goodbye, my daughter.

Thirty-One

I saw you standing there,
Merely feet away.
Talking to another man,
Whose name I cannot say.

You shook your head a little,
And your hair softly swayed.
Although you never looked my way,
I know not why I stayed.

The rest of the people standing there,
Never caught my eye.
I kept coming back to you,
Still, I know not why.

Then you turned and looked at me,
Was truly a surprise.
I think I've never seen such beauty,
As the depth of your brown eyes.

Thirty-Two

An old dog lay beside the rusty fence. His mangy coat was dirty, ragged, and matted. Eyes so full of sorrow, hope as dead as the last loving stroke from any friend.

A scrap of food, a gentle touch, a kind look, and he responds with joy. No longer able to do the things as when he was a pup, he still needs to feel them in his heart.

How can we walk by and show no pity? How can we pass by with no thoughts of ourselves when we, too, have lost much of our youth? When our usefulness has long passed and we can only watch the world pass us by.

Shouldn't we remember when we, too, were young and ran with joy? Bringing smiles to those around us and feeling the warmth of our loved one's arms, remembering when we were everything to those who mattered most to us.

Maybe his life was harsh; maybe it passed him by while others felt the sun upon their faces, and he lived in the shadows. Still, he longs for the kind touch of another, the same as you and I. It takes no longer to smile than it does to ignore.

Take the time to smile at those whose life isn't as good as yours.

Thirty-Three

If I let you hold me while the night is still so young, will you let me go when comes the morning sun? Can you accept what I can give you and not ask for what I can't?

Isn't a moment spent together enough to share if that's all that I can give? Or will you see me in a different light just because I could not stay?

I'll give you all I can and withhold nothing at that time, but the things I cannot give you, you'll never understand.

So I ask again, if I let you hold me for just a little while. Will you let me go? And then give me a smile?

Thirty-Four

Give me your heart,
As I have given you mine.
Share with me your life,
Through the end of time.

Rest in my arms,
Stay by my side.
Promise me your love,
And forever be my bride.

Put your hand in mine,
For the rest of my life.
Standing by my side,
As my loving wife.

Look in my eyes,
And see the love I give.
Forever and ever,
As long as I shall live.

Thirty-Five

The lines of disappoint etched her face,
Signs of joy, there was no trace.

Too many years of trying to stay alive,
Too many years of just trying to survive.

Tracks of tears that long ago fell,
Reminded her daily of her living hell.

No kids, no mate,
A dismal future seemed her fate.

Thirty-Six

My beautiful lady has left me,
She's gone to a better place.
She left me just the other day,
And yet, still, I see her face.

On the day that she left me,
She also took my heart.
I've known that she was leaving,
And that's the saddest part.

For so long, I'd watched her go,
But couldn't change a thing.
I did all I could possibly do,
But help I couldn't bring.

So, goodbye, my love,
You've gone on ahead.
Sadly, I must stay behind,
With a heart that's almost dead.

But precious memories will save me,
And the pain they'll wash away.
My smile will soon return again,
As I live without you each day.

Oh, I'll see you again, my love,
On some much later date.
But until that day finally comes,
I'll accept my lonely fate.

Goodbye, my love. My life is so much less without you in it.

Thirty-Seven

Dark brown and beautiful,
I looked into your eyes.
The bottomless depth they held,
Kept me mesmerized.

When they turned my way,
I was helpless in their gaze.
Wondering what lay behind them,
Haunted me for days.

When they glowed with desire,
I knew it was just for me.
When they shone with pleasure,
'twas impossible not to see.

Of everything about her,
And everything she tries,
The single thing I love the best,
Are those dark brown beautiful eyes?

Arguing with the ignorant is like playing chess with a chicken. You know you'll win, but neither one of them knows they've lost and you've wasted your precious time.

www.ingramcontent.com/pod-product-compliance
Lightning Source LLC
Chambersburg PA
CBHW041122120626

46547CB00019B/2820